This book
belongs to

_____

Jim Henson's
Muppet™
Treasury
Book 1

GROLIER
B O O K S

PARENTS' NOTE: Some of the activities depicted in this book include supplies that may present a danger to certain children. Prior to allowing a child to perform any of the activities in this book, parents should carefully supervise and monitor children, especially young children, so that scissors, small buttons, coins, and other items (such as paperclips) are not handled by very young children and are handled carefully by any other child.

ISBN: 0-7172-8346-1

ILLUSTRATION CREDITS AND ACKNOWLEDGEMENTS: Cover—Tom Brannon; 5-7—Nate Butler; 8-9—Tom Cooke; 10-11—Tom Brannon (border), Tom Cooke (spots); 12-13—Lauren Attinello; 14—Tom Brannon; 15—Lauren Attinello; 16-17—Sue Venning (spot of Gonzo), "Bad hair day" and "All dressed up" from *Bantams In Colour* by the Domestic Fowl Trust, St. Ives, Cornwall; 18-27—Written by H.B. Gilmour, illustrated by Tom Brannon; 28-29—Tom Brannon (border), Tom Cooke (spot); 30—Tom Brannon; 31—Nate Butler; 32-33—Lauren Attinello (illustrations), Tom Cooke (spot); 34-35—Tom Brannon (2 spots), Tom Cooke (illustrations); 36-37—Tom Brannon; 38-39—Sue Venning (spot); "Ponytail," "Hair or headband," "All ashore!" and "Pigtails" from *Fashions in Hair: The First Five Thousand Years* by Richard Corson, Peter Owen Ltd. (London), 1965, "They could use a little trim" from *Old Time Circus Cuts*, edited by Charles Philip Fox, Dover Publications (New York), 1979, "Ah...ah...choo!" *Moustache* by Roger Lax and Maria Carvainis, Quick Fox, a division of Music Sales Ltd. (London), 1979; 40-49—Written by Louise Gikow, illustrated by Lauren Attinello; 50-51—Tom Brannon(border), Tom Cooke (spot); 52—Tom Brannon; 53—Nate Butler; 54-55—Tom Cooke; 56-57—Lauren Attinello; 58-59—Tom Brannon; 60-61—Sue Venning (spot), "I guess he forgot to shave this morning...," photo by J.P. Hutto, "Coffee, tea or meow?" and "It's raining hats and dogs," photos by Harry W. Frees, "I wouldn't want to run into him" and "Can I kiss the bride?" photos by Richard Stack, and "Hare's breakfast" and "Giddyap!" from *Big Bunny Family Album* photos by Harry W. Freese, Ideals Publishing Corp., 1979; 62-71—Written by H.B. Gilmour, illustrated by Mary Bausman; 72-73—Tom Brannon (border), Tom Cooke (spot); 74—Tom Brannon; 75—Nate Butler; 76-77—Tom Cooke; 78-79—Lauren Attinello; 80-81—Tom Brannon; 82-83—Sue Venning (spot), radish photo by Hannah Vanderlaan, carrot photo by Tim Nehls, cabbage photo by Ruth Henry, all other photos by John Faustini; 84-93—Written by Joanne Louise Michaels, illustrated by Tom Cooke; 94-95 —Tom Brannon (border), Tom Cooke (spot); 95—Tom Brannon.

MANUFACTURING ACKNOWLEDGEMENTS: We wish to thank the following for their services: Color Separations, Colotone, Inc.; Text Stock, printed on Union Camp's 70# Williamsburg Offset; Covers, Lehigh Press, Inc.; Printing and Binding, World Color Book Services.

EDITORIAL DEVELOPMENT BY
JIM HENSON PRODUCTIONS, INC.

Publisher	JANE LEVENTHAL
Executive Editor	LOUISE GIKOW
Editor	FRANCESCA OLIVIERI
Art Director	LAUREN ATTINELLO
Designer	RICK PRACHER

PUBLISHED AND MARKETED BY
GROLIER ENTERPRISES INC.

Vice President of Yearbooks	JOHN WEGGEMAN
Product Manager	KATHLEEN C. SCALES
Publisher	BARBARA GREGORY
Associate Editor	CYNTHIA STIERLE

MANUFACTURED BY GROLIER INC.

Director of Manufacturing	JOSEPH J. CORLETT
Senior Production Manager	CHRISTINE L. MATTA
Production Manager	ROSE V. DEMARCO
Production Assistant	J. MARK PETERS

Hi. I'm Kermit, welcoming you to our treasure chest of fun. There are stories, activities, recipes, songs, and lots of other exciting things to do. So join us for a wonderful time!

KERMIT'S ACTIVITIES

This is a great game to play the next time you are on a long car trip. Here are pictures of five different kinds of vehicles. When someone spots one, he or she gets the letter near the vehicle's picture. Keep track with a pencil and paper. When you get the letters *B*, *I*, *N*, *G*, and *O*, yell out "BINGO." The first person to call out "BINGO" wins!

B Truck

I Car

Train

Plane

Fire engine

INDOOR FISHING

What you need:

    1 plain stick or chopstick
    1 piece of string
    1 pipe cleaner, bent into the shape of an *S*
    colored paper for the fish
    round-ended (safety) scissors

Step 1: Tie one end of the piece of string to the stick. This will be your fishing pole.

Step 2: Attach the pipe cleaner to the other end of the string to act as the hook.

Step 3: Cut out fish shapes from the colored paper. Poke a small hole in the top of each fish. Fold back the tops of the fish to make them easier to catch with your hook.

Step 4: Scatter the fish on the floor... and go fishing!

Play with a friend and see who can catch the most fish in the shortest amount of time.

MUPPET POP-UP CARDS

What you need:

    2 pieces of white paper
    round-ended (safety) scissors
    glue
    crayons or felt-tip markers

Step 1: Fold a piece of paper in half.

Step 2: Starting at the fold, cut out a shape. Do not cut it out completely.

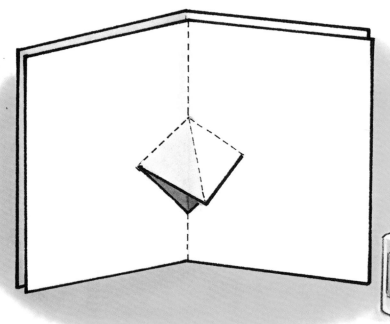

Step 3: Now open it up. Glue the cutout onto the second piece of paper as shown.

Step 4: Decorate the card with crayons or felt-tip markers.

I LoVe YoU xxx ooo

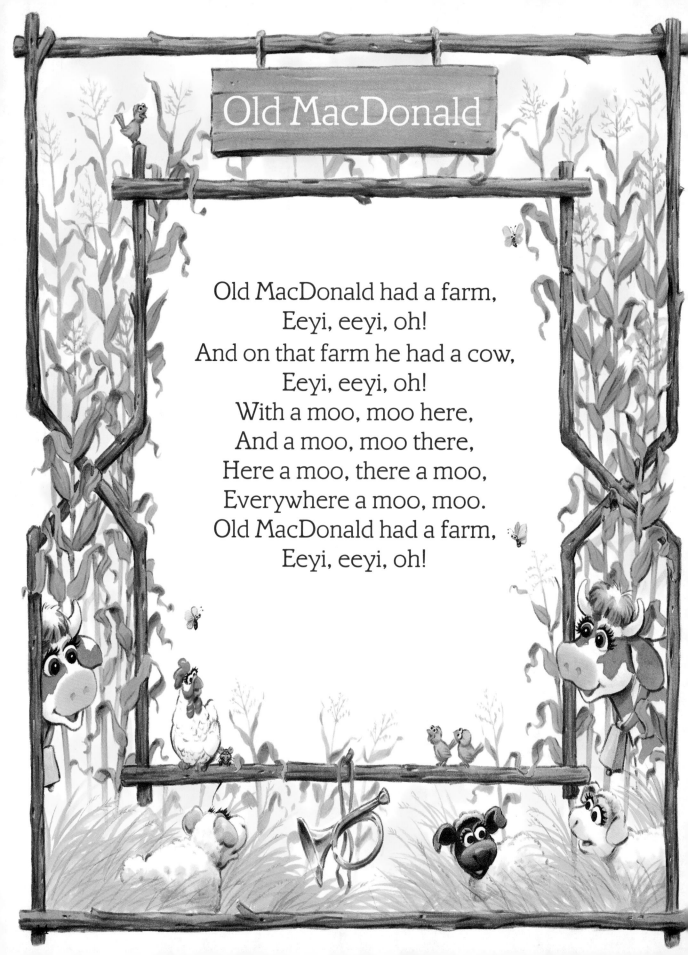

Old MacDonald

Old MacDonald had a farm,
Eeyi, eeyi, oh!
And on that farm he had a cow,
Eeyi, eeyi, oh!
With a moo, moo here,
And a moo, moo there,
Here a moo, there a moo,
Everywhere a moo, moo.
Old MacDonald had a farm,
Eeyi, eeyi, oh!

Hot Cross Buns!

Hot cross buns!
Hot cross buns!
One a penny, two a penny,
Hot cross buns!

If your daughters do not like them,
Give them to your sons.
One a penny, two a penny,
Hot cross buns!

GONZO'S SCRAPBOOK

Favorite

Camilla introduced me to these chicks.

Nice hairdo!

Isn't she beautiful?

All dressed up and nowhere to go!

The car I want to own someday.

Feathered Friends

The Transylvanian naked neck must be related to the giraffe!

I have a yen for Japanese bantams.

This chick is called a Chinese frizzle. Can you see why?

Even Kermit Gets Grouchy

One ordinary morning, for no particular reason at all, Baby Kermit woke up feeling grouchy.

Instead of smiling, he frowned. Instead of being cheerful, he was cranky.

"Kermie has awakened in a grouchy mood," Baby Piggy observed. "Oh, well. It happens to the best of us."

"Let's not disturb him," Fozzie suggested.

So the Babies tiptoed away.

A few minutes later, Kermit peered out from under his blanket and saw that his friends had gone.

"Humph!" Kermit said. "I'd rather be alone, anyway. In fact, I'd rather be far, far away!"

So Kermit packed his suitcase and stepped out into the warm, bright, sunny day. But Kermit didn't even notice the nice weather.

"This is a yucky day," he declared.

"Hey," grumbled a sparrow. "It was a nice day before you came along!"

"Humph!" Kermit sniffed. "I guess I'm just a wet blanket."

Soaked to the skin, Kermit trudged on. As he walked, he felt colder and colder inside. He thought that his friends had frozen him out.

Kermit felt like throwing something as far and as hard as he could. So he reached down to pick up a smooth, black stone.

"Do you mind?" yelped a polar bear. "That's my nose you're trying to grab!"

"Humph," Kermit said grumpily. "Another cold shoulder. Just because I'm not Mr. Nice Frog anymore, nobody wants to have anything to do with me."

Thinking about this made Kermit angry. It really burned him up. He was steaming mad!

Kermit faced a burning desert. Beyond that was a mountain that towered halfway to the sky. It would be the perfect place to be alone.

Kermit hopped across the hot sand from dune to dune. Suddenly, one of the dunes rose up out of the sand.

"Hey! Hop off the hump, okay?" a camel hissed.

"Hump? Humph. I know when I'm not wanted," Kermit replied.

The sun was beginning to set as Kermit started to climb the mountain. Soon he reached the peak.

"Alone at last!" shouted Kermit as night fell.

"Not so fast," bleated a bearded old mountain goat. "You happen to be standing in my living room."

"Humph," Kermit declared. "There's obviously not enough living room here for the two of us. I'll just have to find somewhere else to be alone."

Kermit spotted a moonbeam traveling up toward the stars. He stepped onto it and took the moonbeam to the first meteor he found. There, in the stillness of space, he sat down, with his back to the world—a little lost frog in the universe, sullen, sighing, and, at last, alone.

After a few minutes, Kermit cleared his throat and did what he'd wanted to do all day. He shouted. He stamped his feet and shook his fists. He whined and complained and told the stars how unfair the world was.

"Did that make you feel better?" a voice asked.

Kermit whirled around. He had awakened the moon!

"Well. . . not really," Kermit replied.

"Lighten up. Have some fun," the moon advised. "It's the best cure for grouchiness in the entire solar system."

So Kermit took a ride on a comet roller coaster. He cooled off in a meteor shower. Then he hopped from star to star and made a big splash in the Little Dipper. Soon he was feeling like his old self again.

Kermit turned to thank the moon. But it had already faded. It was time to get back to the nursery. But how?

Suddenly, the star Kermit was standing on began to move.

A bright tail of light exploded from the star. Kermit held on tightly and rode that shooting star all the way to earth.

He landed with a thud right back in his own bed. Fozzie and Piggy wandered over, looking very glad to see him.

"Tell me something," Kermit said to them. "Are you glad to see me just because I'm not grouchy anymore?"

"Of course not," said Fozzie. "We're glad to see you anytime, any way you feel."

"Everyone gets grouchy sometimes, Kermie," Piggy pointed out. "Even you!"

And that's true.

SCOOTER'S & SKEETER'S

Favorite Recipes

Frozen peanut butter pudding is a great dessert idea. Mix up a batch today!

What you need:

1 pint of vanilla frozen yogurt
mixing spoon
1/4 cup of peanut butter
handful of any or all of the
     following: raisins,
     chopped almonds,
     coconut, or other
     mix-in treats
pudding glasses

Step 1: Let the yogurt stand at room temperature until soft.

Step 2: When it is soft enough, use a spoon to blend in the peanut butter and any of the other ingredients you are using.

Step 3: Spoon mixture into pudding glasses and put into the freezer to chill.

For advanced cooks:

Spoon the mixture into a pie shell and . . . *presto*! You have a frozen peanut butter pudding pie!

Q: What outlaw was famous for his practical jokes?
A: Billy the Kidder.

Q: Why did the cowboy put a blanket over the dog's tail?
A: He wanted a covered waggin'.

Q: What do cowboys do when they come to a lake?
A: They have a row-deo.

Q: What did the western acorn want to be when it grew up?
A: Annie Oaktree.

My favorite food is cookies.

I like to dance.

My favorite clothes are my lavender gloves.

My favorite picture is of Kermie and me.

I like to listen to happy songs.

Hi. I'm Piggy. Welcome to my tea party.
What are some of your favorite things?

PIGGY'S ACTIVITIES

PAPER SNOWFLAKE

What you need:

1 square piece of white paper
round-ended (safety) scissors
crayons, felt-tip markers, or glitter
ribbon or string

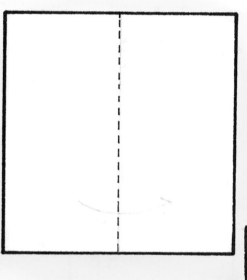

Step 1: Fold paper in half.

Step 2: Fold paper in half again as shown.

Step 3: Fold the top corner down to the bottom opposite corner. Now you have a triangle.

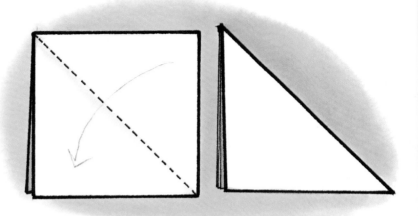

Step 4: Cut out small shapes on all three sides of your triangle.

Step 5: Unfold the snowflake. You can decorate it with crayons, felt-tip markers, or glitter if you like. Thread the string or ribbon through one of the openings to hang your snowflake up.

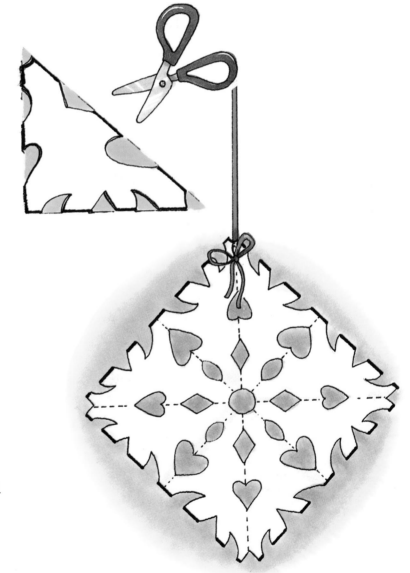

DANDELION JEWELRY

What you need:

dandelions (You can find them growing on lawns, in parks, and even through cracks in the sidewalk. Ask permission before you pick them from a neighbor's yard.)

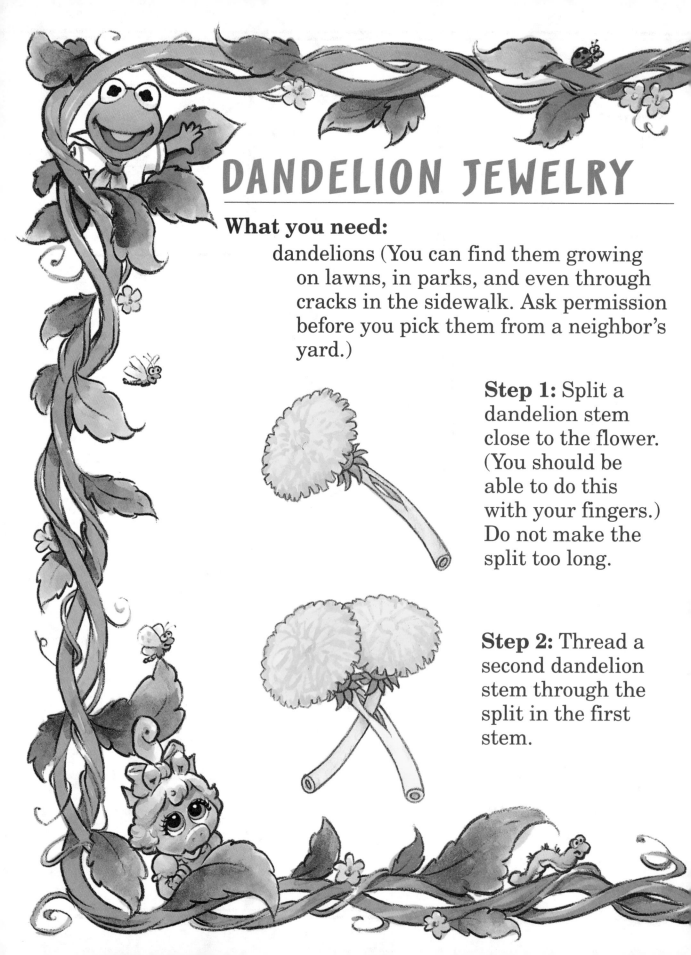

Step 1: Split a dandelion stem close to the flower. (You should be able to do this with your fingers.) Do not make the split too long.

Step 2: Thread a second dandelion stem through the split in the first stem.

Step 3: Split the second stem and thread another dandelion through that split. Do this again and again.

Step 4: When you've made the chain long enough, split the last stem and thread the very first flower through it. Snip off any excess stems.

Dandelions can be sticky! So be sure to wash up when you're finished.

Mary, Mary,
Quite Contrary

Mary, Mary, quite contrary,
How does your garden grow?

"With silver bells
and cockle shells,
And pretty maids
all in a row."

Row, Row, Row Your Boat

Row, row, row your boat,
Gently down the stream.
Merrily, merrily, merrily,
merrily,
Life is but a dream.

For a fun sing-along, try singing this song in a round with a friend. When the first singer reaches the end of the first line, the other singer begins the song at the beginning.

GONZO'S SCRAPBOOK

Heaps of Hair

These people should think about getting new barbers.

Nice ponytail!

You should have seen her *before* the haircut!

Ah . . .

Do you think anything is nesting in there?

Is this hair or a headband?

Baby Piggy's Night at the Ball

Baby Piggy was planning a wonderful costume ball. It was time to invite the guests.

"Kermie, would you like to come to my ball?" Piggy asked sweetly. "All of the dolls will be there. There will be music and dancing and lemonade and cupcakes."

"Gee, Piggy," answered Kermit. "I promised to play pirates with Fozzie. Maybe another time."

"I'm not doing anything," Gonzo piped up. "May I come?"

"No way, Bluebeak," Piggy sniffed. "You'd only get your nose into everything and make a mess."

Piggy took all of her dolls down from the shelves. There were baby dolls and tin soldiers, and then there was Oliver—a funny, floppy, stuffed clown.

"We don't want to be late," she told the dolls. "So let's put on our costumes. I'm going to be a fairy princess. What are you going to wear, Oliver?"

"I'm already dressed for the ball!" replied Oliver. "I'm going as a clown. After all, that's what I always am!"

"He shouldn't be allowed to come," said one of the dolls. "He's always doing silly things."

Piggy disagreed. "All of the other dolls are coming, and so should he."

The ballroom was beautiful! A crystal chandelier hung from the ceiling, and there were flowers everywhere and a huge table loaded with treats.

Piggy was snacking when she noticed a crowd gathered around the table. She looked over. Oliver was up to his usual tricks, trying to balance a bowl of chocolate ice cream on his nose!

As Piggy watched, the bowl began to wobble. Then it fell, splashing chocolate ice cream all over the place.

"Oh, Oliver! Look at the mess you've made!" Piggy gazed down at the spilled ice cream.

Oliver hung his head. "I'm sorry," he said. "I didn't mean to."

Later, Piggy and a handsome frog were doing the frog trot when she noticed Oliver again. This time, he was practicing his somersault . . . and he was headed straight for the orchestra!

"Watch out!" Piggy cried. But it was too late. Oliver had rolled right into the violin section.

"You're spoiling the whole ball," Piggy said. "Why don't you go home? You've made a mess of everything."

Oliver just stood there. A tear trickled slowly down his cheek. "I'm sorry. I didn't mean to," he whispered.

When Piggy saw Oliver crying, the messes he had made didn't seem very important.

"Don't worry," she said gently. "It doesn't matter. We'll clean everything up. You're my friend—and that's what counts."

When Baby Piggy looked around, she found she was back in the nursery. There was Gonzo standing by himself. Piggy remembered what she had said to him when he'd asked to come to the ball.

"Gonzo?" said Piggy. "The costume ball is still going on, and I was wondering if you'd like to come after all."

"Wow! I sure would!" Gonzo grinned. "Thanks! I can wear my new space helmet!" He brushed off his shoes and gave his helmet a quick polish.

Then Gonzo led Piggy out to the middle of the floor for a dance.

Gonzo was trying out his super-duper loop-de-looper twirl when he landed on Piggy's toes.

"I'm sorry," he said, blushing. "I didn't mean to."

"That's all right, Gonzo," said Piggy. "It doesn't matter. You're my friend—and that's what counts!"

SCOOTER'S & SKEETER'S

Favorite Recipes

Surprise your friends and family with this tangy treat—crazy cubes!

What you need:

- 1 cup of orange juice
- 1 cup of cranberry juice
- 1 cup of apple juice
- plastic pitcher
- large bowl
- 1 small package of frozen raspberries, thawed
- large wooden spoon
- 2 ice cube trays
- plastic wrap and toothpicks (optional)

Step 1: Mix the three different juices in a pitcher.

Step 2: In a large bowl, mash the thawed raspberries with a spoon. Pour into the pitcher of juice.

Step 3: Pour juice/fruit mixture into the ice cube trays. Cover with plastic wrap and insert a toothpick into each ice cube if you plan to eat them like mini-ices. Leave them as is to use as yummy ice cubes in juice or water.

Step 4: Place in freezer for four hours.

BABY FOZZIE'S

JOKES

Q: Why did the gladiators go on a trip?

A: Because they were part of the Roamin' Empire.

Q: Who conquered the world with jelly?

A: Alexander the Grape.

Q: What famous ruler made a monkey of himself?

A: King Henry the Ape.

Q: What did the weatherperson say when the emperor asked about the weather?

A: "Hail, Caesar."

Q: Who is Rowlf's favorite woman in history?

A: Joan of Bark.

FOZZIE'S ACTIVITIES

CRAYON RUBBINGS

What you need:

    white paper
    masking tape
    flat objects that have some
        interesting texture
    crayon

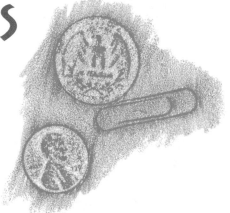

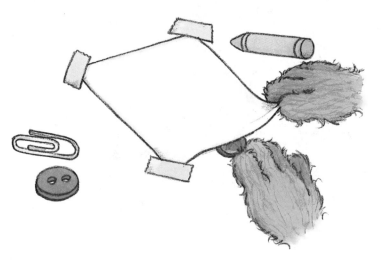

Step 1: Tape three corners of the paper to a work table. Put the first object under the paper. Now tape down the fourth corner.

Step 2: Gently begin rubbing over the object with the crayon.

Have a friend guess what the object is *before* you finish rubbing it.

SAVE-A-SNOWMAN

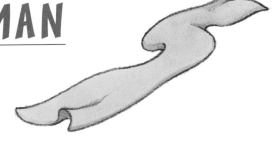

What you need:

    snow
    raisins
    piece of fabric

Step 1: Make two snowballs. One should be bigger than the other one.

Step 2: Place the smaller snowball on top of the bigger one. Use raisins for a face and buttons, and fabric for the scarf.

Step 3: Put your creation into the freezer and remove it in the middle of the summer. There you have it—a snowman when it sizzles!

(Be sure to get a grown-up's permission to keep your snowman in the freezer.)

SOCK PUPPETS

What you need:

        old sock
        pencil
        paper towel roll
        needle and thread or glue
        2 buttons
        yarn scraps
        fabric scraps
        felt-tip markers or glitter (optional)

Step 1: Put your hand in the sock and have an adult mark with a pencil where the eyes, nose, and hair should be.

Step 2: Put the paper towel roll inside the sock before you begin sewing so that you don't sew the sides of the sock together.

Step 3: Sew or glue on buttons for the eyes, yarn for the hair, and fabric for the tongue and ears. You can also use felt-tip markers or glitter. Have fun!

Twinkle, Twinkle, Little Star

Twinkle, twinkle, little star,
How I wonder what you are.
Up above the world so high,
Like a diamond in the sky.
Twinkle, twinkle, little star,
How I wonder what you are.

Twinkle, twinkle, little star,
How I wonder what you are.
As your bright and tiny spark
Lights the traveler in the dark.
Though I know not what you are,
Twinkle, twinkle, little star.

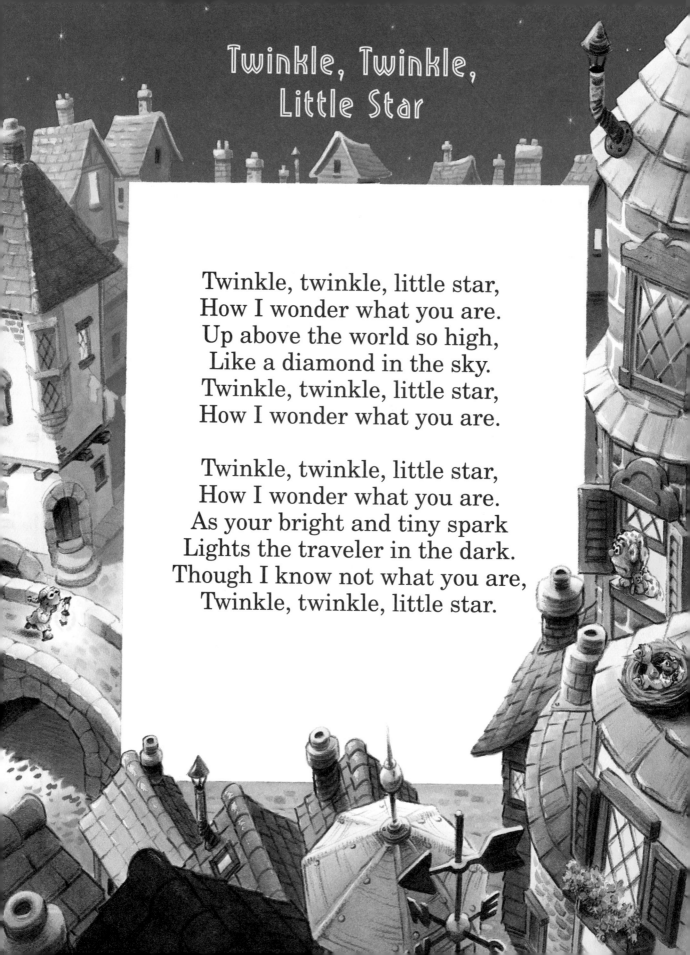

SHE SELLS SEASHELLS

She sells seashells
by the seashore.

See the seashells
that she sells.

How many seashells
does she sell?

The shells that she sells
are swell, I'm sure.

(Try saying this one
five times fast.)

GONZO'S SCRAPBOOK

Peculiar Pets

These are not your everyday house pets.

I guess he forgot to shave this morning....

May I kiss the bride?

I wouldn't want to run into
him on the high seas!

Hare's breakfast!

It's raining hats and dogs.

Coffee, tea, or meow?

Giddyap!

If I Were Just Like Kermit

Baby Kermit had a cold. His nose was red. His eyes looked bleary. Nanny said he had to stay in bed. Baby Fozzie decided to cheer up Kermit with a joke. "What's green and red and has to stay in bed?" he asked.

"Ah doh doh," said Kermit. He was trying to say "I don't know."

"*You* are!" Baby Fozzie exclaimed. "You are green. Your nose is red. And today you have to stay in bed." Kermit did not laugh. He just rolled over and went back to sleep.

Fozzie walked away, sighing to himself. "I tried to cheer up my friend Kermit," he muttered, "and, instead, I put him to sleep. If I were sick, Kermit would know exactly what to do to make *me* feel better."

Suddenly, Baby Fozzie snapped his fingers. "If I do just what Kermit would do, I *can* make him feel good!" Fozzie closed his eyes. "Kermit is so kind. He would probably fix me a great big breakfast in bed. So that's what I'll do."

Fozzie found some butter and six eggs. He dropped three of the eggs on the floor and began to scramble the others in a frying pan. Then he put two nice thick slices of bread in the toaster and went to hunt for jam. The eggs and toast began to burn. Fozzie finally found the jam behind a pile of cans that toppled off a shelf. "Oh, dear!" cried Fozzie. "I'd better find a mop and pail to tidy up this awful mess. I have to be helpful because that is exactly what Kermit would do."

Determined to be as helpful as Kermit would be, Fozzie ran to the sink and turned on the water. Then off he went to find a pail and a mop. He hurried as fast as he could, but the water was faster than he was. By the time Baby Fozzie returned to the kitchen, there was enough water on the floor for a seafaring bear to go sailing.

"What would Kermit—who is daring—do in a case like this?" Fozzie wondered aloud, trying hard to stay afloat. "Why, Kermit would climb aboard the pail and sail off on an exciting adventure," he decided.

So he scrambled into the pail. The mop made a very fine oar. He peered through his spyglass in search of a distant shore.

All of a sudden, Baby Fozzie gulped, and then he dropped his spyglass. He couldn't believe what he'd just seen. It was huge. It swam like a fish. Its tail was spiky and green. Fozzie wished he were back in the nursery.

"What would Kermit do now?" Fozzie asked himself. "He would be brave and polite."

So brave Fozzie sailed closer to the creature. "Excuse me," he said politely to the beast. "It's a pleasure to meet you." Then Fozzie smiled. It was only a baby sea monster that had been taking a bubble bath.

It had been a lovely adventure, but Fozzie wished he were back on dry land. "What would clever Kermit do if he were tired of bobbing around in a pail?" Fozzie wondered. "He certainly wouldn't fuss or shout. Kermit would just reach overboard, pull the plug, and let the water out!"

As Fozzie was reaching overboard, the pail tipped. Poor Fozzie fell out, and down he went. And down. And down.

Beneath the water, Fozzie thought he saw the plug. He swam toward it with all his might.

The next thing Fozzie knew, he was staring at Nanny's shoes.

"Fozzie, why are you trying to swim on the nursery floor?" Nanny was asking. "Oh, my! You've got a lump on your head. I'd better get you right into bed."

When Kermit woke up, he was feeling much better. He found Baby Fozzie lying next to him.

"Fozzie, what happened to you?"

"Well, I thought that if I were just like you, I'd know how to make you feel better," said Fozzie, sighing. "But I'm better at being myself than I am at being like you."

"That's okay," said Kermit, smiling. "I like you just the way you are!"

SCOOTER'S & SKEETER'S

Favorite Recipes

It's time to make gingerbread people! Be sure to have a grown-up help you use the oven and stove.

What you need:

1 baking sheet
1 tablespoon of butter or shortening
2 cups of all-purpose flour
1 teaspoon of ground ginger
1 teaspoon of ground cloves
1 teaspoon of nutmeg
1 teaspoon of baking soda
mixing bowl
5 tablespoons of molasses
1/4 cup of light brown sugar
4 tablespoons of butter
saucepan
1 egg, beaten
rolling pin
gingerbread people cookie cutters
raisins and icing tubes for decorations

Step 1: Preheat the oven to 350° F. Grease the baking sheet with the tablespoon of butter or shortening. Sift all dry ingredients into a mixing bowl.

Step 2: Place the molasses, sugar, and the rest of the butter into a saucepan and heat until melted. Put the melted ingredients into the bowl with the dry ingredients and add the beaten egg. Mix all of the ingredients together to form a ball of dough.

Step 3: Sprinkle some flour on your work space and the rolling pin so that the dough will not stick to them. Using the rolling pin, roll out the dough until it is about 1/8-inch thick. Cut out the cookies with gingerbread people cookie cutters. Place the shapes onto the greased baking sheet. Put raisins onto the cookies for buttons.

Step 4: Bake the gingerbread people for about 20 minutes, or until they are brown around the edges.

Step 5: When the gingerbread people have cooled, use icing tubes to decorate them.

BABY FOZZIE'S JOKES

Q: Why did the chicken cross the road?
A: To get to the other side!

Q: Why did the rooster cross the road?
A: He was following the chicken!

Q: Why did the turtle cross the road?
A: It was the chicken's day off.

Q: Where does a 600-pound gorilla sit?
A: Anywhere it wants to!

Q: What do you get if you cross a cow with an insect?
A: A moo-squito!

This is my favorite plant. I entered it in a science fair.

My favorite sandwich is anchovies and liverwurst.

This is my favorite chicken sculpture.

This is my favorite mold collection.

This is my favorite collection of polka-dot rubber bands.

Hi, I'm Gonzo. And these are my favorite weird things. What are some of your favorite things?

GONZO'S ACTIVITIES

HALLOWEEN MASKS

It's fun to make your own mask for Halloween. Here's a cat mask you can try. Use your imagination to come up with other types of masks.

What you need:
round-ended (safety) scissors
paper plate
construction paper
glue
crayons
yarn

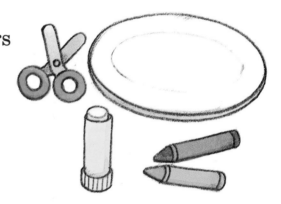

Step 1: Cut two holes in the paper plate for the cat's eyes. Then cut a hole for the mouth. Make sure you can see easily through the eyeholes.

Step 2: Cut three triangles out of a piece of construction paper—one for the nose and two for the ears. Cut six thin strips for the whiskers.

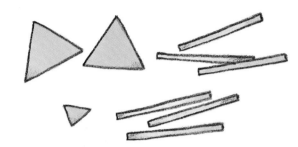

Step 3: Glue down the whiskers as shown in the picture. Then glue on the nose and the ears.

Step 4: Using crayons, yarn, and anything else you want, decorate your cat mask.

Step 5: Make a hole on each side of the mask. Tie a piece of yarn through each hole. Have someone else tie the mask around the back of your head.

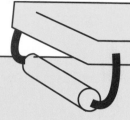

MUNCH A

Make your lunch box a fun box with these creative lunch ideas. Have a grown-up help you cut out all the pieces for these neat sandwich creations.

Sandwich house: Cut a sandwich (of your choice) into a house shape. Use a carrot circle and thin carrot sticks for the sun, and cheese pieces for the door and windows.

Sandwich face: Spread peanut butter on two round crackers; top with raisins to make the eyes. Add freckles. A wedge of cheese can be the nose, and a carrot stick—the mouth. Two apple slices make great ears.

MASTERPIECE

Sandwich man: Cut a sandwich into rectangles, one for the head, one for the body, and four thin ones for arms and legs. Use peanuts or raisins for the eyes and buttons.

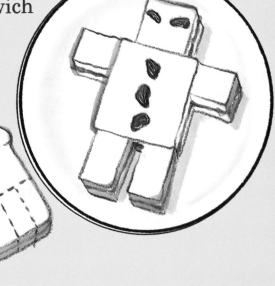

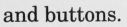

Sandwich ship: Cut your sandwich into three triangles—one large, two small. Use the large triangle for the boat, and the two smaller ones for sails. Pretzel sticks make good masts, and Goldfish crackers are great fish.

Ring around the Rosie

Ring around the rosie,
A pocket full of posies.
Ashes! Ashes!
We all fall down!

The cows are in the meadow,
Huddled all together.
Thunder! Lightning!
We all jump up!

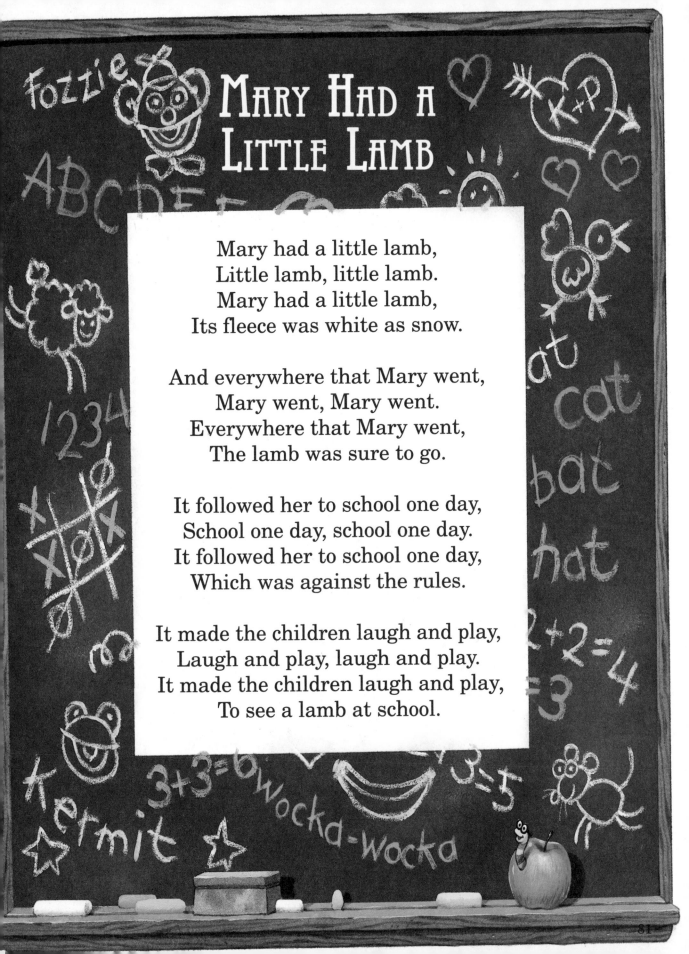

MARY HAD A LITTLE LAMB

Mary had a little lamb,
Little lamb, little lamb.
Mary had a little lamb,
Its fleece was white as snow.

And everywhere that Mary went,
Mary went, Mary went.
Everywhere that Mary went,
The lamb was sure to go.

It followed her to school one day,
School one day, school one day.
It followed her to school one day,
Which was against the rules.

It made the children laugh and play,
Laugh and play, laugh and play.
It made the children laugh and play,
To see a lamb at school.

This is the biggest Kohlrabi I've ever seen—in fact, it's the only one.

Nice hat!

That's one big radish.

Baby Gonzo's Treasure Hunt

One rainy morning, the Muppet Babies were eating breakfast.

"Gee," Gonzo said glumly. "It's raining so hard that Nanny will never be able to take us to the amusement park today. I'm bored."

"Use your imagination," Kermit suggested. "Just look what's on the back of this box of Golden Treasure cereal. It's a real pirates' map!"

"That isn't a real map," said Gonzo. "It's only a game on a cereal box."

Kermit shook his head. "Take a closer look."

Gonzo picked up the box and peered at the map.

Suddenly, Gonzo felt the floor moving. When he looked up, he was no longer in the nursery. He was on the deck of a huge pirate ship anchored off a tropical island. Around him stood his pirate crew. They were all pointing at the map in Captain Gonzo's hands.

"This map means silver...gold...jewels...real treasure!" bellowed the first mate, Mr. Kreegle. "And it's a pirate's duty to hunt for buried treasure!"

"Well... if you say so," Gonzo said, and shrugged his shoulders.

The pirates all climbed into their longboat and rowed to shore.

"It says here," said Mr. Kreegle, looking at the map, "that we first have to cross the Oozyfenoozy Swamp to get to the treasure."

Before they reached the other side of the swamp, Goldtooth Dan got stuck in quicksand, Pee Wee was nearly carried off by a giant pink flamingo, and a crocodile tried to take a bite out of Peg Leg's peg leg.

"Now the treasure map says we've got to climb to the top of Mount Never Rest," Mr. Kreegle declared.

During the climb, three of the pirates almost fell off a cliff, Cutlass Kurt had a shouting match with a big brown bear, and Cross-eyed Jack began an avalanche when he stubbed his toe on a boulder.

The map next led them to the wide and dangerous Slamazon River. Captain Gonzo and the pirates built a sturdy raft and set off across the water. But the churning rapids caught them and whirled them downstream. The next thing they knew, they were going over a fifty-foot waterfall. Four of the pirates were swept overboard.

"At least they're all good swimmers," Mr. Kreegle observed as he helped the last of the pirates back onto the raft.

"Shiver me timbers!" Gonzo yelled. "This is really exciting!"

The pirates finally reached a sandy beach. "Here!" Mr. Kreegle shouted. "We're supposed to dig for the treasure at the *X*!"

"I think I've hit something!" Captain Gonzo yelled. "Dig faster!"

Before you could say "Yo-ho-ho," the pirates had dug up an old treasure chest.

Captain Gonzo took a deep breath and lifted up the lid of the chest. All of the pirates peered inside.

"Ah!" sighed Mr. Kreegle. "This is the richest treasure in the world."

Gonzo stared into the chest. "What are you talking about?" he asked in amazement. "The only thing in here is Golden Treasure cereal!"

"That's right!" cheered Mr. Kreegle. "And we're hungry! We never stopped for breakfast this morning!"

Back in the nursery, Gonzo was finishing his cereal.

"Zowie, Kermit!" he said. "You were right. I just had the greatest pirate adventure ever!"

"Not bad for a rainy morning," Kermit said. "And you thought you were going to be bored."

"Bored?" Gonzo swallowed his last spoonful. "No way! Now that I've finished breakfast, I'm ready for another adventure. Would anyone like to join me?"

SCOOTER'S & SKEETER'S
Favorite Recipes

Roasted pumpkin seeds are delicious and easy to make! Be sure to have a grown-up help you use the oven.

What you need:

large spoon
pumpkin
bowl
3 teaspoons of olive oil

baking or
cookie sheet
paper towel
salt

Step 1: Preheat the oven to 350° F. After scooping the seeds and pulp out of your pumpkin, pick out the seeds.

Step 2: Rinse the pumpkin seeds and then pat them dry.

Step 3: Put the seeds into a bowl. Pour oil over the seeds and mix.

Step 4: Spread the seeds out on a cookie sheet.

Step 5: Bake the seeds until they are lightly browned, about 10 minutes.

Step 6: Drain the seeds on a paper towel, sprinkle them with salt, and they are ready to eat!

BABY FOZZIE'S

JOKES

Q: Why shouldn't you tell secrets in a cornfield?
A: Because it's full of ears!

Q: What do cows wear in Hawaii?
A: Moo-moos!

Q: How do you make time fly?
A: Throw the clock out the window!

Q: What time is it when the clock strikes thirteen?
A: Time to get the clock fixed!

Q: What do you get if you cross a cow with a rabbit?
A: A hare in your milk!

Q: Why did the boy throw his toast out the window?
A: He wanted to see the butter fly!